Hello, Hello!

BY **Miriam Schlein**

ILLUSTRATED BY **Daniel Kirk**

Simon & Schuster Books for Young Readers
New York   London   Toronto   Sydney   Singapore

When two lions meet,
how do they say hello?

They rub their foreheads together,
and make a humming noise . . .
like this . . . HMMMM . . .

That's how two lions say hello.
Mmmmmm. HELLO.

**How do polar bears
who meet in the snow
say hello?**

They walk around one another,
then sit down
and grab each other's jaws.
That's how polar bears
in the snow say HELLO.

**How do chimpanzees
in the trees
say hello?**

They reach out
and touch hands.

Sometimes they say hello
with a hug
or a kiss.
HELLO. HELLO.

**When two wolves meet,
how do they greet
one another?**

**They wave their tails
and lick one another's faces.
Sometimes they lift one paw.**

That's how wolves who meet
say **HELLO**.

How do beavers in the pond say hello?
They swim toward one another,
and touch noses
for a second . . . like this . . .
HELLO.

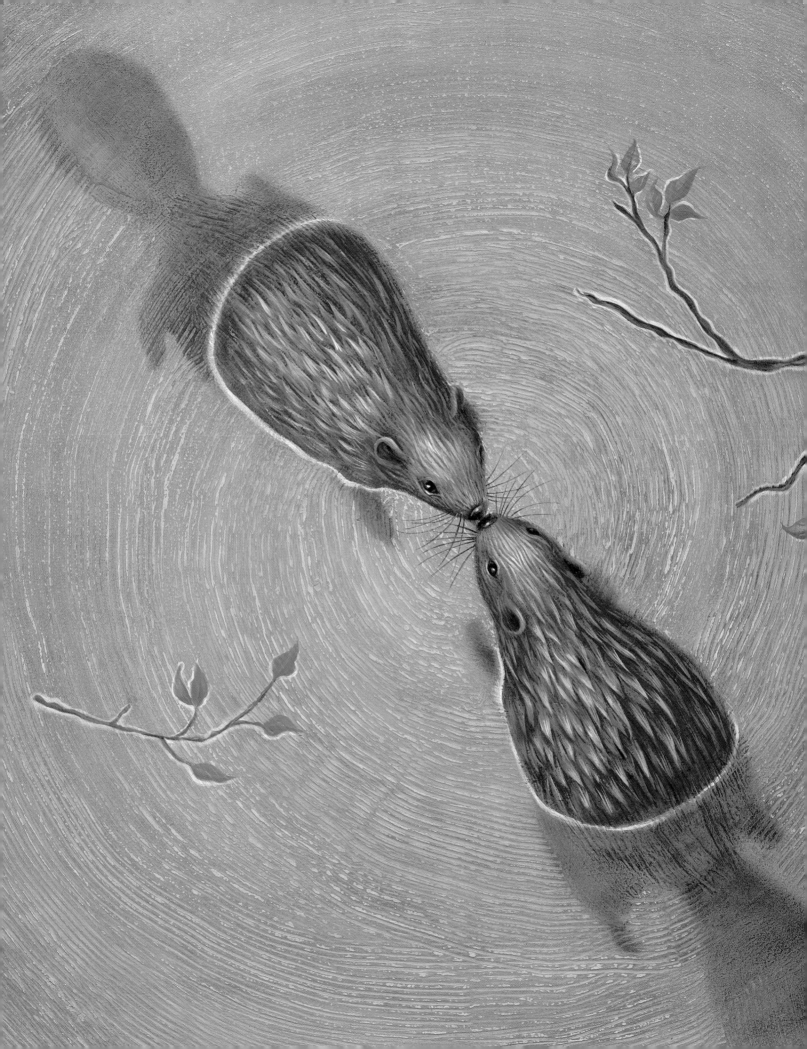

**Do zebras who meet
on the plain say hello?
Oh, yes.**

They stretch out their necks,
and sniff each other's noses,
and make little chewing movements.

**Then they back off
with a quick little JUMP!**

That's the special zebra way
to say HELLO!

This is what two penguins do:
They face each other, toe-to-toe,
and wave their wings
s . . . l . . . o . . . w . . . l . . . y . . .
as they lift their faces
up toward the sky.

Then they sing a little duet.
It sounds something like this:
KRONK . . . KRONK . . . KRAAAUUNK!
HELLO.

There are lots of ways
elephants say hello.
Elephants are very, very,
very, very friendly.
They touch trunk tips.
Or they put the tips of their trunks
in one another's mouths.

Sometimes they
click their tusks.
CLICK. CLICK.

Then they twine their
trunks together.
HELLO. HELLO.

How do you say hello?
With a smile?
With a wave?

With a shake of the hand?
With a bow?

With a hug?
With a kiss?
HELLO!

To Julia and Russell
—D. K.

SIMON & SCHUSTER BOOKS FOR YOUNG READERS
An imprint of Simon & Schuster Children's Publishing Division
1230 Avenue of the Americas, New York, New York 10020
Text copyright © 2002 by Miriam Schlein
Illustrations copyright © 2002 by Daniel Kirk
All rights reserved, including the right of reproduction in whole or in part in any form.
SIMON & SCHUSTER BOOKS FOR YOUNG READERS is a trademark of Simon & Schuster.
Book design by Paul Zakris
The text for this book is set in 22-point Folio Bold.
The illustrations are rendered in oil paint on textured paper.
Printed in Hong Kong
2 4 6 8 10 9 7 5 3 1

Library of Congress Cataloging-in-Publication Data

Schlein, Miriam.
Hello, hello! / by Miriam Schlein ; illustrated by Daniel Kirk.
p. cm.
ISBN 0-689-83435-7
1. Animal communication—Juvenile literature.
[1. Animal communication.]   I. Kirk, Daniel, ill. II. Title.
QL776 .S326 2002
591.59—dc21
00-045061